D0274646

CATS

MAYLING IS.

THE SONGS FROM THE MUSICAL BY

ANDREW LLOYD WEBBER

BASED ON 'OLD POSSUM'S BOOK OF PRACTICAL CATS' BY

T. S. ELIOT

FABER MUSIC LTD
3 QUEEN SQUARE   LONDON WC1

CHAPPELL INTERNATIONAL MUSIC PUBLISHERS LTD

8.99

Cats is recorded on a Polydor double record album (CATX 001)

Also available:

Cats, the Book of the Musical, with many coloured production photographs and contributions by Andrew Lloyd Webber, Valerie Eliot, Trevor Nunn, Gillian Lynne and the designer John Napier. Published by Faber & Faber and The Really Useful Company.

CONTENTS

I began setting *Old Possum's Book of Practical Cats* to music late in 1977, partly because it is a book I remember with affection from my childhood and partly because I wanted to set existing verse to music. When I have written with lyricists in the past we have agreed together the dramatic structure, but for the most part the lyrics have been written to the music. So I was intrigued to see whether I could write a complete piece the other way round.

Very luckily *Old Possum* contains verses that are extraordinarily musical; they have rhythms that are very much their own, like the 'Rum Tum Tugger' or 'Old Deuteronomy' and, although clearly they dictate to some degree the music that will accompany them, they are frequently of irregular and exciting metre and are very challenging to a composer.

My first plans were for a concert anthology, and it was with this in mind that some of my settings were performed in the summer of 1980 at the Sydmonton Festival. Mrs Eliot fortunately came to the concert and brought with her various unpublished pieces of verse by her husband, including 'Grizabella: the Glamour Cat.' The musical and dramatic images that this created for me made me feel that there was very much more to the project than I had realized. In Trevor Nunn I found a collaborator with a taste for tackling theatrical problems that most people would consider insoluble. Together we worked out a dramatic structure for a full evening, helped by further unpublished Eliot material that Mrs Eliot kindly provided and by the many references to cats in the the main body of his writing. The show, as its form emerged, gave me an exciting opportunity to compose dance music and I was fortunate to be guided through the unfamiliar world of choreography by someone as experienced as Gillian Lynne.

I enjoyed working on *Cats* as much as on any show on which I have worked. My gratitude will be undying to Valerie Eliot without whose encouragement it could never have taken its present form.

Cats opened at the New London Theatre on May 11th 1981. This folio contains most of the music from the London production as recorded on the Polydor double record album. For reasons of space there are inevitably some omissions, principally the longer dance sections and the extended setting of 'The Pekes and the Pollicles'. There are also some small alterations and cuts, notably in the Prologue 'Jellicle Songs for Jellicle Cats'.

T. S. Eliot wrote the *Old Possum* poems in a series of letters to his godchildren and it is almost certain that their parents were just as much the intended recipients of the poems as those children. I hope that the music of *Cats* achieves the sense of fun that abounds in Eliot's verse.

ANDREW LLOYD WEBBER

A Note on the Text

Most of the poems comprising *Old Possum's Book of Practical Cats* (1939) have been set to music complete and in their originally published form; a few have been subject to a minor revision of tense or pronoun, and eight lines have been added to 'The Song of the Jellicles'. However, some of our lyrics, notably 'The Marching Song of the Pollicle Dogs' and the story of 'Grizabella', were discovered among the unpublished writings of Eliot. The prologue is based on ideas and incorporates lines from another unpublished poem, entitled 'Pollicle Dogs and Jellicle Cats'. 'Memory' includes lines from and is suggested by 'Rhapsody on a Windy Night', and other poems of the Prufrock period. All other words in the show are taken from the Collected Poems.

TREVOR NUNN

Overture

Music by
ANDREW LLOYD WEBBER

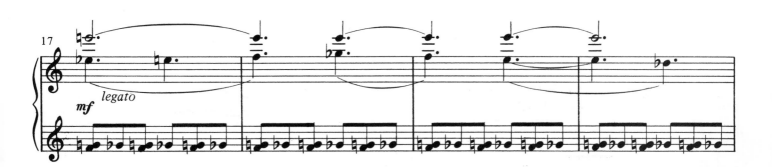

Jellicle Songs for Jellicle Cats

Music by
ANDREW LLOYD WEBBER

Text by
TREVOR NUNN and RICHARD STILGOE
after T.S. ELIOT

Jel-li-cle songs for Jel-li-cle Cats. Can you sing at the same time, in more than one key, Du-

F#   F#/A#   B   C#7   Gm   Ab   Ab/G

-ets by Ros-si-ni and waltz-es by Strauss? And can you (as cats do) be-

F   F7   Gm   Ebmaj7

-gin with a C that al-ways tri-um-phant-ly brings down the house?

Ab7   Db   D7   G

Jel-li-cle Cats are queen of the nights Sing-ing at as-tro-no-mi-cal heights,

G   C/G   G   D7/G

Han - del - ling pie - ces from the Mes - si - ah, Hal - le - lu - jah, __ an - ge - li - cal choir. __

G   D/G   G   D

Meno mosso [♩ = 82]

mp The mys - ti - cal di - vin - i - ty of un - a - shamed fe -

Bb   Bb   F

- lin - i - ty *f* Round the ca - the - dral rang "Vi - vat". Life to the

Bb   F   Bb   Eb   Bb   Ab

e - ver - last - ing cat, *mf* Fe - line, fear - less, faith - ful and true To

Eb/G   F   Bbm   Bbm7

18

-cle songs for Jel-li-cle Cats, __ Jel-li-cle songs for Jel-li-cle Cats, __ Jel-li-cle songs for Jel-li-cle Cats.

Bb Eb   Eb/G   Ab9   Bb Eb   Eb/G   Ab

Slower, in free tempo
SOLO

There's a man o-ver there __ with a look of sur-prise, __ As much as to say, __ well now

Slower (colla voce)

Ebm   Fb   Db

how a-bout that? __ Do I ac-tual-ly see __ with my own ve-ry eyes __ A

Eb m   Cb♮7   Fb

CHORUS (whisper)

man who's not heard of a Jel-li-cle Cat? __ What's a Jel-li-cle Cat? __ What's a Jel-li-cle Cat? __

A   Bb   Eb

Attacca 'The Naming of Cats'

The Naming of Cats

Music by
ANDREW LLOYD WEBBER

Text by
T.S. ELIOT

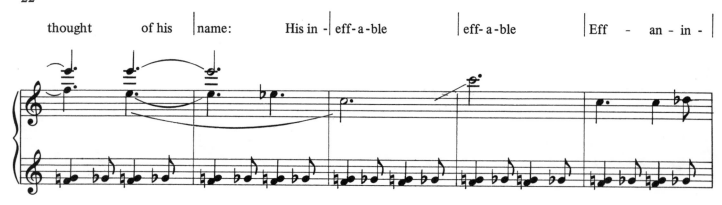

The Invitation to the Jellicle Ball

Jellicle Cats come out tonight,
Jellicle Cats come one come all:
The Jellicle Moon is shining bright —
Jellicles come to the Jellicle Ball.

Jellicle Cats meet once a year
At the Jellicle Ball where we all rejoice,
And the Jellicle leader will soon appear
And make what is known as the Jellicle choice —

When Old Deuteronomy just before dawn,
Through a silence you feel you can cut with a knife,
Announces the cat who can now be reborn
And come back to a different Jellicle life.

For waiting up there is the Heaviside Layer,
Full of wonders one Jellicle only will see,
And Jellicles ask, because Jellicles dare:
Who will it be? Who will it be?

The Old Gumbie Cat

Music by
ANDREW LLOYD WEBBER

Text by
T.S. ELIOT

Legato (a Glenn Miller flavour) [♩ = 104]

ev - en cre - a - ted a Bee - tles' Tat - too. __

The Rum Tum Tugger

Music by
ANDREW LLOYD WEBBER

Text by
T.S. ELIOT

Bustopher Jones: the Cat about Town

Music by
ANDREW LLOYD WEBBER

Text by
T.S. ELIOT

Dignified [♩ = 104]

CHORUS

Bus-to-pher Jones____ is not skin and bones,____ In fact he's re - mar - ka-bly fat.____
cat we all greet____ as he walks down the street____ In his coat of fas-ti - di-ous black:____

He does-n't haunt pubs,____ he has eight or nine clubs,____ For
No com-mon place mou-sers____ have such well-cut trou-sers____ Or

he's the St. Jame-s's Street Cat!____ He's the

such an im-pec-ca-ble back.____

36

So, much in this way, pass-es Bus-to-pher's day,— At one club or an-o-ther he's found.— It can be no sur-prise that un-der our eyes— He has grown un-mis-tak-a-bly round.— He's a twen-ty-five poun-der, or I am a boun-der, And he's put-ting on weight ev-ery day:— But I'm

BUSTOPHER JONES   CHORUS   BUSTOPHER JONES

Mungojerrie and Rumpelteazer

Music by
ANDREW LLOYD WEBBER

Text by
T.S. ELIOT

[♩. = 84]

MUNGOJERRIE and RUMPELTEAZER

Mun - go-jer - rie and Rum - pel-tea - zer, we're a no-tor-i-ous cou-ple of cats. As
Mun - go-jer - rie and Rum - pel-tea - zer have a ve-ry un-us-u-al gift of the gab. We are

Dm6   Dm6

knock-a-bout clowns, quick change co-me-di-ans, tight-rope walk-ers and ac-ro-bats We
high-ly ef-fi-cient cat-bur-glars as well and re-mark-a-bly smart at a smash and grab. We

C6   G7

1st time only

have an ex-ten-sive re-pu-ta-tion. We make our home in Vic-tor-i-a Grove: That is

Dm6   Dm6

(both times)

fa - mi - ly will say: 'It's that hor - ri - ble cat!__ Was it Mun - go - jer - rie or

F

Rum - pel - tea - zer?' And most of the time they leave it at that.

A7

Eb9   A7   Eb9   A7   Eb7

A7   Ebm

Mun - go - jer - rie and Rum - pel - tea - zer have a

46

Old Deuteronomy

Music by
ANDREW LLOYD WEBBER

Text by
T.S. ELIOT

50

The Awefull Battle of the Pekes and the Pollicles

OF THE AWEFULL BATTLE
OF THE PEKES AND THE POLLICLES
Together with some Account
of the Participation
of the Pugs and the Poms, and
the Intervention of the Great Rumpuscat

The Pekes and the Pollicles, everyone knows,
Are proud and implacable passionate foes;
It is always the same, wherever one goes.
And the Pugs and the Poms, although most people say
That they do not like fighting, yet once in a way,
They will now and again join in to the fray
And they
      Bark bark bark bark
      Bark bark BARK BARK
Until you can hear them all over the Park.

Now on the occasion of which I shall speak
Almost nothing had happened for nearly a week
(And that's a long time for a Pol or a Peke).
The big Police Dog was away from his beat —
I don't know the reason, but most people think
He'd slipped into the Wellington Arms for a drink —
And no one at all was about on the street
When a Peke and a Pollicle happened to meet.
They did not advance, or exactly retreat,
But they glared at each other, and scraped their hind feet,
And started to
      Bark bark bark bark
      Bark bark BARK BARK
Until you could hear them all over the Park.

Now the Peke, although people may say what they please,
Is no British Dog, but a Heathen Chinese.
And so all the Pekes, when they heard the uproar,
Some came to the window, some came to the door;
There were surely a dozen, more likely a score.
And together they started to grumble and wheeze
In their huffery-snuffery Heathen Chinese.
But a terrible din is what Pollicles like,
For your Pollicle Dog is a dour Yorkshire tyke.

There are dogs out of every nation,
The Irish, the Welsh and the Dane;
The Russian, the Dutch, the Dalmatian,
And even from China and Spain;
The Poodle, the Pom, the Alsatian
And the mastiff who walks on a chain.
And to those that are frisky and frollical
Let my meaning be perfectly plain:
That my name it is Little Tom Pollicle —
And you'd better not do it again.

And his braw Scottish cousins are snappers and biters,
And every dog-jack of them notable fighters;
And so they stepped out, with their pipers in order,
Playing *When the Blue Bonnets Came Over the Border*.
Then the Pugs and the Poms held no longer aloof,
But some from the balcony, some from the roof,
Joined in
To the din
With a
      Bark bark bark bark
      Bark bark BARK BARK
Until you could hear them all over the Park.

Now when these bold heroes together assembled,
The traffic all stopped, and the Underground trembled,
And some of the neighbours were so much afraid
That they started to ring up the Fire Brigade.
When suddenly, up from a small basement flat,
Why who should stalk out but the GREAT RUMPUSCAT.
His eyes were like fireballs fearfully blazing,
He gave a great yawn, and his jaws were amazing;
And when he looked out through the bars of the area,
You never saw anything fiercer or hairier.
And what with the glare of his eyes and his yawning,
The Pekes and the Pollicles quickly took warning.
He looked at the sky and he gave a great leap —
And they every last one of them scattered like sheep.

And when the Police Dog returned to his beat,
There wasn't a single one left in the street.

The Song of the Jellicles

Music by
ANDREW LLOYD WEBBER

Text by
T.S. ELIOT

CHORUS *(spoken in rhythm)*

Jel - li - cle Cats come | out to - night, | Jel - li - cle Cats come | one come all: The
Jel - li - cle Moon is | shin - ing bright: | Jel - li - cles come to the | Jel - li - cle Ball.

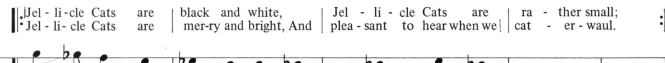

Jel - li - cle Cats are | black and white, | Jel - li - cle Cats are | ra - ther small;
Jel - li - cle Cats are | mer-ry and bright, And | plea - sant to hear when we | cat - er-waul.

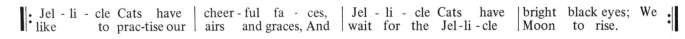

Jel - li - cle Cats have | cheer-ful fa - ces, | Jel - li - cle Cats have | bright black eyes; We
like to prac-tise our | airs and graces, And | wait for the Jel-li - cle | Moon to rise.

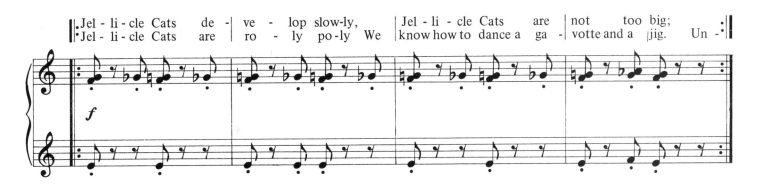

Jel - li - cle Cats de - ve - lop slow-ly, Jel - li - cle Cats are | not too big;
Jel - li - cle Cats are | ro - ly po -ly We | know how to dance a ga - | votte and a | jig. Un -

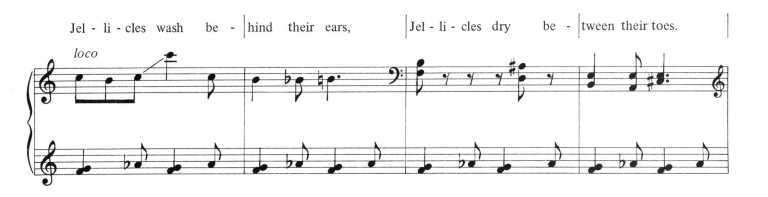

- til the Jel - li -cle | Moon ap - pears We | make our toi-lette and | take our re - pose:

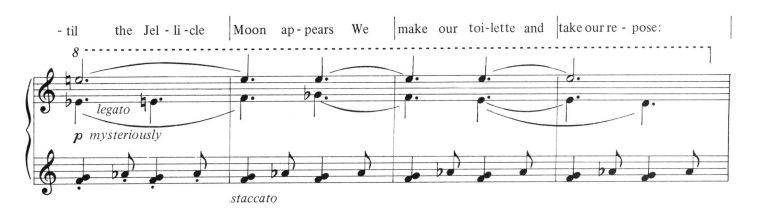

Jel - li - cles wash be - | hind their ears, | Jel - li - cles dry be - | tween their toes.

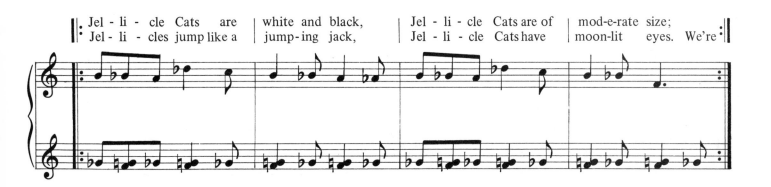

Jel - li - cle Cats are | white and black, | Jel - li - cle Cats are of | mod-e-rate size;
Jel - li - cles jump like a | jump-ing jack, | Jel - li - cle Cats have | moon-lit eyes. We're

quiet e - nough in the mor - ning hours, We're quiet e - nough in the af - ter - noon, Re -

- ser- ving our terp - si - chor- e - an powers To dance by the light of the Jel - li -cle Moon.

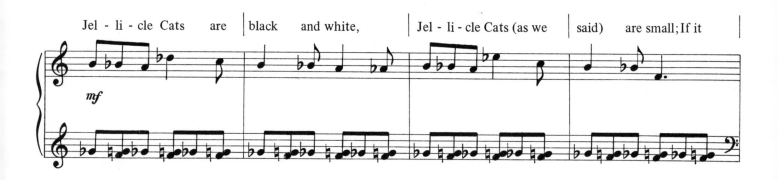

Jel - li - cle Cats are black and white, Jel - li - cle Cats (as we said) are small; If it

hap-pens to be a stor - my night We will prac-tise a ca-per or two in the hall. If it

Here follows 'The Jellicle Ball'.

Grizabella: the Glamour Cat

Music by
ANDREW LLOYD WEBBER

Text by
T.S. ELIOT

SOLO

Slow [♩ = 68]

p She haunt- ed ma-ny a low re - sort_ near the gri - my road of

Tot-ten-ham Court;_ She flit-ted a-bout_ the No - man's Land_ From The

Ris - ing Sun_ to The Friend at Hand. And the post - man sighed, as he

Bbm   F7   F7   Db   Db   Ebm6   Db/F   Gb   Cb   Bbm

Was Gri - za - bel - la, the Gla - mour Cat!

Ebm   Bbm/F   Em Abm

rall.

The Moments of Happiness

The moments of happiness . . .
We had the experience but missed the meaning,
And approach to the meaning restores the experience
In a different form, beyond any meaning
We can assign to happiness . . .
. . . the past experience revived in the meaning
Is not the experience of one life only
But of many generations — not forgetting
Something that is probably quite ineffable . . .

(from T.S. Eliot 'The Dry Salvages' in *Four Quartets*)

Gus: the Theatre Cat

Music by
ANDREW LLOYD WEBBER

Text by
T.S. ELIOT

GUS (Sung reprise)

And I once crossed the stage on a telegraph wire,
To rescue a child when a house was on fire.
And I think that I still can much better than most,
Produce blood-curdling noises to bring on the Ghost.
I once played Growltiger, could do it again . . .

attacca 'Growltiger's Last Stand'

Growltiger's Last Stand

Music by
ANDREW LLOYD WEBBER

Text by
T.S. ELIOT

barge at Mole - sey lay. _____ All in the bal - my moon-light it lay rock-ing on the tide, And Growl-
gone to wet his beard; And his bo - sun, Tumble Bru - tus, he too had stol'n a - way: In the

Ab Fm Ab Ebm Fm Gb Ab

1

- tig - er was dis - posed to show his sen - ti - men - tal side. Growl-ti-ger's
yard be-hind the Li - on he was

Ab Gb Ebm Gb Fm Ebm Fm Db Db

2 *poco più mosso*

prowl-ing for his prey. In the fore-peak of the ves - sel Growl - tig - er sat a - lone, Con-cen -

poco più mosso

Ebm Fm Db Cb Cb maj7 Cb6

- tra - ting his at - ten - tion on the La - dy Grid-dle-bone. And his raf - fish crew were sleep-ing in their

Fb Fbmaj7 Fb6 A Amaj7

sam-pans cir-cled round, And yet from all the e-ne-my there was not heard a sound. The

foe was armed with toast-ing forks and cru-el carv-ing knives, And the lov-ers sang their last du-et, in dan-ger of their lives.

rall.

a tempo

Presto [♩ = 140]

Then Gilbert gave the signal to his fierce Mongolian horde; With a frightful burst of fireworks the Chinks they swarmed aboard.

ff a tempo

Presto [♩ = 140]

Then Grid - dle - bone she

*Here follows 'The Ballad of Billy M'Caw' (p. 74)

The Ballad of Billy M'Caw

Music by
ANDREW LLOYD WEBBER

Text by
T.S. ELIOT

toe of her boot Or as like-ly as not put her fist through your eye. But

B7   E   G#7

when we was hap-py, and just a bit dry, Or when we was thir-sty, and

C#m   E7   A   F#m

rall.

just a bit sad, She would rap on the bar with that cork-screw she had And say

B7   A7   B7

a tempo

'Bil-ly! Bil-ly M'-Caw! _____ Come give us a tune on your pas-to-ral flute!' And
'Bil-ly! Bil-ly M'-Caw! _____ Come give us a tune on your mo-ley gui-tar!' And

E   C#7   F#m   B

78

Skimbleshanks: the Railway Cat

Music by
ANDREW LLOYD WEBBER

Text by
T. S. ELIOT

Lively [♩. = 98]

E   C#m/E   F#m7/E   B/E   E   C#m/E   F#m7/E   B/E

CHORUS

Skim - ble - shanks, the Rail - way Cat, _____ the

E   C#m/E   F#m7/E   B/E   E   C#m/e   F#m7/E   B/E

SKIMBLE

Cat of the Rail - way Train!   There's a

E   B7/E   F#m/E   E   C#m/E   F#m7/E   B/E

Vivace [♩ = 144]

whis - per down the line at e - le - ven thir - ty - nine When the
say that by and large it was me who was in charge Of the

Vivace [♩ = 144]

E   B/D#   C#m   E/B

SKIMBLE
(2nd time)

82

Macavity: the Mystery Cat

Music by
ANDREW LLOYD WEBBER

Text by
T.S. ELIOT

89

coat is dus - ty from ne-glect, his whis - kers are un-combed. He

sways his head from side to side, with move - ments like a snake; And

when you think he's half a- sleep, he's al - ways wide a- wake. Mac -

Chorus

- a - vi - ty, Mac - a - vi - ty, there's no one like Mac - a - vi - ty. For
- a - vi - ty, Mac - a - vi - ty, there's no one like Mac - a - vi - ty, There

Cm   Cm/Eb   F7   D7/F#   (G7)

Mr. Mistoffelees

Music by
ANDREW LLOYD WEBBER

Text by
T.S. ELIOT

SOLO You ought to ask Mr. Mistoffelees!
The Original Conjuring Cat.
The great-est ma-gi-cians have some-thing to learn__ From

Mis-ter Mis-tof - fel-ee-s's Con-jur-ing Turn.__ Pre-sto! And we all say:

CHORUS
Oh! Well I ne-ver! Was__there e-ver a cat so cle-ver as Ma-gi-cal Mis-ter Mis-tof-

1.
- fel-ees!

2. SOLO
- fel-ees!
He is quiet, he is small, he is black From his
His manner is vague and a-loof, You would

ears to the tip of his tail;___ He can creep thru' the ti-ni-est crack, He can
think there was no-bo-dy shy-er, But his voice has been heard on the roof When

B♭   F   F   A♭

walk on the nar-row-est rail. He can pick a-ny card from a pack, He is
he was curled up by the fire. And he's some-times been heard by the fire, When

B♭   A♭   B♭   A♭

e-qual-ly cun-ning with dice; He is al-ways de-ceiv-ing you in-to be-liev-ing That he's
he was a-bout on the roof (At least we all heard___ that some-bo-dy purred) Which is

D♭   F   B♭   F

on-ly hunt-ing for mice. He can play a-ny trick with a cork Or a spoon and a bit of fish paste; If you
in-con-test-a-ble proof Of his sin-gu-lar ma-gi-cal powers: And I've known the fam-ily to call Him

cresc. poco a poco

E♭   C7   C7   C7

Memory

Music by
ANDREW LLOYD WEBBER

Text by
TREVOR NUNN
after T.S. ELIOT

[Grizabella is chosen to go to the Heaviside Layer.]

The Journey to the Heaviside Layer

Music by
ANDREW LLOYD WEBBER

Text by
T. S. ELIOT

Grandly [♩ = 104]

Up up up past the Rus-sell Ho-tel,___ Up up up up___ to the Hea -vi- side Layer.

CHORUS

Up up up past the Rus-sell Ho-tel,___ Up up up up___ to the Hea -vi- side Layer.

rall

* For complete instrumental, take in bars 61 to 88 of Overture (pp. 8 –10)

The Ad-dressing of Cats

Music by
ANDREW LLOYD WEBBER

Text by
T.S. ELIOT

-bout the town is in - clined to play the clown. A - gain I must re -

Bb   Eb/Bb Bb   Cm/Bb Bb   F   Eb   Bb   Eb/Bb

- mind you that   A ___ dog's a dog, a cat's a

Bb   Gm   Bb/F   Eb   Bb/D Cm   Bb   F   Eb

OLD DEUTERONOMY

cat.   mf With cats, some say, one rule is

legato
mp

Bb   Eb/Bb

rall.

true: Don't speak till you are spo - ken to. My -

Bb   C7   F   C7   F

CHORUS

Printed by J. B. Offset (Marks Tey) Limited, Colchester, Essex.